Do You Know Why So Many Relationships Fail?

The Secret to Maintaining a Meaningful Relationship

DR. JEFFERY L. WALKER

authorHOUSE®

AuthorHouse™
1663 Liberty Drive
Bloomington, IN 47403
www.authorhouse.com
Phone: 1 (800) 839-8640

Published by AuthorHouse 04/27/2017

ISBN: 978-1-5246-8722-9 (sc)
ISBN: 978-1-5246-8721-2 (e)

Print information available on the last page.

This book is printed on acid-free paper.

Contents

About the Author

Dr. Jeffery L. Walker, a native of Omaha, Nebraska has written several books on human behavior. He is a visionary with a passion for assisting others to alleviate or at best, mitigate their internal conflict so they can clear the dust that hinders their vision. Dr. Walker has 22 years of experience working with a diverse population in Chemical Dependency and Mental Health Counseling. He is an author, life coach, educator and motivational speaker on various topics such as; anger, domestic violence, relationship conflict, and racism in the 21st century. He obtained his Associates of Applied Science (A.A.S.) in Criminal Justice/Law Enforcement, Inver Hills Community College, Inver Grove Heights, Minnesota. Rasmussen School of Business, Diploma, St. Paul, Mn. Bachelor's (B.A.) in Psychology, Metropolitan State University, St. Paul, Minnesota. Master's (M.A.) in Human Relations from the University of Oklahoma. Doctorate (Ed.D.) in Higher Education with a concentration in Psychology from College of Saint Mary, Omaha, Nebraska. Dr. Walker believes that the environment is not stressful it is how we perceive it.

Acknowledgement

I would like to give a shout-out to all the amazing people who completed my survey on **Do You Know Why So Many Relationships Fail?** I have interviewed over 100 people, who consisted of 50 women and 50 men from all nationalities, and I used their lived experiences to complete this book. Everyone who participated in the survey appeared to be very open and honest with answering the survey questions in a timely and faithful manner. I found the comments interesting what men and women had to say about each other and their past relationships. Without the input of so many fabulous people, perhaps this book may not have been composed. I thank you all from the bottom of my heart . . . One love!

Dedication

This book is dedicated to the millions of people who have been hurt by someone they romantically loved. The book is for those who have struggled to make sense of this thing called **relationship.** We all have experienced relationship conflict, but the key is, "did you wait for the storm to pass or did you learn to dance in the rain." What I am conveying, did you try to work through your relationship conflict or did you decide to move onward to a new relationship? Nevertheless, I dedicate this book to those who are still experiencing emotional cardiac arrest (a broken heart) from a failed relationship. Herein lies hope!

The Emotional Pilot Light

When the emotional pilot light goes out,
the relationship is in serious trouble!

Relationship Complaints by Men and Women

Men

Through my survey, I discovered that many men have **seven primary complaints** about women. These complaints have a universal spend to it because it represents five ethnic groups, Whites, Blacks, Native Americans, Hispanics, and Asian American men. The seven complaints are as follows:

- Nagging
- Alcohol and Drug Abuse
- Relationship Deception (cheating)
- Instant Gratification
- Controlling
- Manipulative
- Laziness

Women

I also discovered many women have multiple complaints as well, a matter of fact; they have **thirteen primary complaints** about men. These complaints are from women from all ethnic groups as well.

- Controlling
- Manipulative
- Alcohol and Drug Abuse
- Domestic Violence (verbal and physical)
- Relationship Deception (cheating)

- Dishonesty
- Laziness
- Self-Centeredness
- Fatherhood Deception (running from their biological responsibilities)
- Watching television and ignoring their significant others needs
- Not having enough money to support their lifestyle
- Not listening
- Limited communication skills

The bottom line is when a relationship contains any form of deception problems will occur. After examining the above complaints from men and women, I have concluded both genders need to make a psychological incision and carefully review their moral fabric. In doing so, you can begin to understand how you are emotionally wired as a human being and learn to stay within the circumference of morality.

Warning!

Please read with caution because the contents of this book are a reality of the here and now!

Introduction

Did you know two out of three relationships expire before reaching their full potential? Many Americans are wondering why their relationships are so difficult to maintain. It is not a complicated situation if you examine the importance of what I call the **emotional seed.** In this reality book, you will discover eight essential characteristics such as; respect, honesty, commitment, human touch (intimacy), openness, creativity, communication, and love style. These eight elements are paramount to discovering, maintaining, and living a successful life with your soul mate. Ninety percent of relationships lack substance, which is the emotional foundation necessary to give birth to a beautiful and rewarding life together. However, most couples do not know how to apply **emotional nourishment** to sustain a healthy relationship.

Are you ready to journey with me and examine the pitfalls that apparently have the potential to blow out your **emotional pilot light?** If so, continue to read and go on a psychological journey and recapture your past relationships. I know you will discover some critical mistakes that smothered the growth of your emotional seed. It is the time you learn how to administer an **emotional autopsy.** Without it, you will carry the same negative baggage into a new relationship and duplicate the same critical mistakes that caused your previous relationship to fail. I do not wish for this to happen to you again. Therefore, I encourage you to read this book very carefully, and as you are reading, please consider your morals, values, and belief system. In a later chapter, I will explain the meaning of the **eight essential love ingredients.**

Are you ready to master the recipe for true unconditional love?

If you are, then let the journey begin!

The Socialization Process

Every human being searches for a sense of belonging. The problem with this process is you have the tendency to connect with the wrong people. Most of the stresses and strains you encounter derive from your socialization process. Building a rapport with the opposite sex or the same sex is time-consuming. In developing friendships and relationships, people look for certain characteristics that are magnetic to your own. During your lifetime, you accumulate many friends and relationships, but as time progresses, you start to notice negative traits that cause you to stray away.

Men and Women Campaigning for Love

It is safe to assume many people look for a mate in all the wrong places such as in bars, at parties, and utilizing online dating services. Another way most people meet a partner is through friends that introduce them to a person they believe would be a good match. In my opinion, this type of matchmaking can have a harmful effect because the matchmaker is using **magical thinking**, meaning they think they know what a person is searching for in a mate. Also, you need to realize blind dates are often a mistake as well for an individual is missing the key factor that elicits your emotional desires and that element is physical attraction. You must remember, beauty is in the eyes of the beholder.

Physical appearance is the first form of attraction, but often it is misleading. People have the propensity to focus on the external and ignore the internal characteristics where substance lies. It is true that "beauty is in the eyes of the beholder, [but we must also realize] beauty is only skin deep." We live in a **cute society** because you are always searching for perfect bone structures in one's physiognomy (the layout of someone's face). This physical desire is very damaging

1

since you have a magnetic instinct to merge with a person that is pleasing to the eyes. Everybody would like to be with someone who satisfies their visual desires, but this is superficial as you cannot see substance you must feel it. The obsession with looks destroys one's ability to socialize with people who may not fall under the **umbrella of cuteness**. It is vital that people stop looking for physical perfection and focus on personality and character traits. When you learn how to do that, you will begin to come to terms with what a holistic relationship entails.

Once you determine someone is good looking, there is a unique process you go through called **sizing a person up**, meaning, I would like to get with him or her. Most people do not think about anything else, and right away they go into a fantasy mold about how one may kiss, or create an illusion of how they may be in bed. Your senses become aroused, and then you formulate thoughts about an individual before you know anything about them, be honest, am I right? The bottom line is, you learn in the nest (home environment) to judge a person based on looks alone. People are so caught up on personal appearance that nothing else matters, and you go into a relationship base on physical attraction, which is equivalent to judging a book by its cover, is that not true? The question is, why do people disregard someone who is undesirable to the human eye? What is it about physical attraction that blinds individuals from penetrating the external and examining the internal? Here's an interesting note; how do you suppose sightless people grow in love when they cannot see each other? They rely on personality traits such as the eight essential ingredients discussed in full detail in a later chapter. Also, food for thought, when sightless people marry they usually mate for life. Now take a minute and think hard about this concept. I bet that you have never thought about this.

It is a real story, but the name is fictitious. Susan, a 24-year-old beautiful woman, met this handsome young man one day at the shopping mall. They spoke briefly and exchanged phone numbers which are consistent with physical attraction. When Susan returned home, she immediately called her best girlfriend and told her about this good looking dude she had just met. She went on to describe him by quoting visible facts such as; "girl he is so fine, and he smells like a million dollars." He has a good job and drives a brand new BMW. Susan's girlfriend was just as excited as she was and told Susan to keep her posted on the progression of the relationship. To make a long story short, Susan went on several dates with this man over a short period and found herself mesmerized by his suave gentle personality.

For the first month they were doing very well, so Susan thought until she started to notice some character defects in him, but by this time, it was far too late because she had already given her precious gift (her body) away. Susan saw a massive change in his behavior and his pattern of phone calling changed drastically. When calling him in the evening hours, he would never answer his cell or home phone. One night through frustration and curiosity, she decided to go to his house and discovered something that hurt her. She witnessed him coming out of his house with another woman, and they were kissing each other and holding hands. Susan went home and cried her eyes out because she thought this handsome man was her soul mate.

Susan waited until the next day to call him and asked what did you do last night and his reply, "I was tired baby, so I slept all evening." Susan stated, "you are a d★★★ liar because I came by your house and saw you kissing another woman." It broke Susan's heart, so she hung up on him and cried a river and never called him again. Matter of fact, he never called her either. A week later her girlfriend called and asked about her relationship with this handsome man. Susan replied, "girl this guy was playing me like a fiddle, and he is a pathological liar. I had no clue this gorgeous looking man was so crazy and deceptive," and this is a prime example of focusing on the external and not penetrating the internal. The truth of the matter is, looks can be very rewarding but also deceiving, so please do not forget this important message.

It is necessary during the mating and dating process you stay on the spiritual side of a relationship until you develop a holistic rapport. One of the biggest mistakes couples make is they move too fast into the desert of a relationship, which is sex. Once you exchange DNA, (releasing of body fluids) it is no longer just a friendship, it is now a relationship because friendship is platonic, but some people are comfortable having a friendship with sexual benefits. It is confusing for friendship doesn't require sexual stimulation, but a relationship does. With that said, once you determine it is a relationship, you go through a transformation that will bring about pleasure or pain. Remember many men have sex to release, whereas, most women have sex to bond. I know most men will disagree with my ideology, but that is because it is the gospel. To the contrary, men and women think differently about relationships. Therefore, let's examine some hard core facts about **campaigning for love.**

First, men and woman are programmed to look for physical perfection. It is human nature to search for a man who is attractive and a woman who has a sexy anatomical structure. Many men are naturally prospectors, and what is a prospector? Someone who is searching for gold, (sex) and who has the gold, the woman. Yes, I said it, women can be extremely magnetic. I am keeping it real since most men look at women through objective lens, meaning they look at the size of her breast and a★★. Please excuse my linguistic French, but it is what it is. I know because I am a man, and displayed the same behavior until taking a moral inventory of myself and discovered how a man is designed. To the contrary, it changed my perspective on how I view women. Now I see women as equal to men and treat them with the utmost respect.

Most men focus on the external characteristics of a woman because this is what they learned in the nest. From childhood to adulthood, some males are programmed to recognize the physical ornaments a woman displays to the world. But, keep in mind women are guilty too, which is wrong as two left shoes. Although males and females capture this visual observation, men tend to be the aggressor. If you were to sit and listen to men talk about women, you would be amazed about some of the statements you would hear them say. For example, the first words that come out of their mouths, she is good looking and has a nice a★★ on her. Wow! I sure would like to have sexual relations with her. I know this sounds gross, but I am giving you sheer facts about how most men view women. However, it is important to note not all men look at women through objective lens, but let's keep it real, most men do. In fact, it is rare a man does not focus on the anatomical structure of a woman and a woman does not focus on how good looking a man is.

Both genders are equally guilty of misconstruing visual stimulation. It might explain why women are receiving facelifts, breast implants, tummy tucks and butt enhancements. On the other hand, many men are spending large amounts of money on fashionable clothes, jewelry, cars and material objects to create an illusion that is magnetic to the female eye. Cold thang (interesting)! What are you doing to each other? Have people become so superficial that they will do anything to satisfy their pseudo ego and pride.

When men and women stop looking at each other as sexual objects and focus more on their spiritual being, they can begin to view each other as an equal. Please note, I am not putting anyone down. I am shooting from the hip (telling the truth) about how men and women observe each other. In my opinion, a man or a woman is not fully developed until sex is no longer their primary drive. Consequently, women are similar to men when it comes to physical attraction. Matter of fact, women are probably more conditioned to judge a book by its cover oppose to men. Women have the tendency to search for the perfect man that suits her visual desires. Physical attraction is related to both genders. It's the number one topic you will hear women discuss when they are socializing with their friends. For example, you will hear women say, "girl he is so good looking," and some women will notice his muscled body, and say, "he appears to be well endowed."

For some reason, people want to be seen with a good looking man or woman so they can show the world the beauty of their mate. Let's be real some men and women may not have the natural good looks or money but can create a beautiful external illusion, which is designed to fake out the human eye. Therefore, are you beginning to understand the pitfalls of external illusion? If you are, then my mission thus far is accomplished.

Growing in Love

Dating is an age old romantic concept, matter of fact, it dates back to the biblical days. In my opinion, dating is designed to impress or in some cases depress an individual. Dating can set you up for relationship failure because the behavior is well groomed to influence the man or woman. When a man is attracted to a woman, he tells her she is very attractive and would she be kind enough to go out to dinner with him. If the woman reciprocates his attraction, she will most likely say yes if she is not involved with someone, but in some cases, she still may say yes. What happens next is superficial regarding setting a date up for artificial stimulation. You are probably wondering what I mean by artificial stimulation (bullsh★★). I am merely saying that dates are designed to impress the other person, in other words, you are on your best behavior, right? People are not what they appear to be on their first encounter, so it is crucial not to rush into the physical side of love too soon. I use the phraseology of growing in love because you don't fall in love; you grow in love. When you grow in love, it gives an individual the opportunity to plant the emotional seed. On the other hand, falling in love is a misrepresentation of the power of this thing called love. However, growing in love is authentic and time-consuming as it gives both individuals the opportunity to nourish the relationship.

Dating

In the dating game, the rules are terribly misleading because the pressure is primarily for the man to be the aggressor and provide the expense of dating. Although some women understand the Dutch theory, meaning they share the cost of the date with the man and many women disagree with this concept. Most women expect men to pay for everything during the dating season and if they don't pay they view them as cheap. However, some women do not know that after a few dates men turn into an accountant (count how much money they have spent on the dates). It might explain why men tend to want sex after one or two encounters since they feel they deserve it due to the amount of money spent on the dates. This ideology is how most men think and this is terribly twisted.

To my male readers, you are probably saying this is not true, come on now, keep it real. Earlier, I mentioned the dating game can set you up for failure for the reason that both parties are on their best behavior. Therefore, it is a challenge to distinguish if a person is real or not. During the dating process, you are overwhelmed by the kindness represented by both individuals, and this is misleading for couples are attracted to artificial stimulation. This type of magnetic power can fool you as human beings are masters at masking their true self in fear of a person rejecting them. Nevertheless, the majority of people have the tendency to display conduct that is kind to your heart. The downfall is if their actions are not real, the authentic character of the person you desire will start to unfold in due time. When this occurs, usually it is too late since you have already developed an emotional rapport.

As the dating game continues, you will start to notice character defects in your person of interest. What I mean by this is once you exchanged your personal gift (having sex) the level of desire tends to change in most cases but not all. Theoretically, people do not change unless there is a stimulus (something that causes activity). Individuals become so mesmerized by the external glow (appearance) they develop psychological cataracts (can't see the situation clearly), that causes many dating couples to miss vital cognitive and behavior clues. Perhaps this may explain why countless men and women experience emotional cardiac arrest (broken heart). I have heard many women talk about how their relationships hurt them immensely as they witnessed behaviors they did not see in the first stage of their dating. Women throughout the United Sates repeatedly state, "men tend to change after they get what they want, and that is sex." However, many men deny this fact.

Men and women date for different reasons for they are each searching for certain characteristics that accommodate their image of the perfect man or woman. The problem with preconceived desires is people get caught up with expectations, which can bring about disappointment. Due to the fact, that dating can be very exciting and rewarding; you must not forget dating is set up to impress your emotional appetite to find a suitable mate. However, there are three phases in dating, excitement, commitment, and complacency which are vital to successful dating. Let's break down each component so you understand the emotional developmental stages of **growing in love.**

The **excitement phase** is when you first meet each other and discover the attraction is mutual. This phase is very arousing because both individuals are doing their very best to impress each other. Remember, the first form of attraction is physical, so once you make the connection the emotional journey begins. In the **second phase** is when you make a conscious decision to date this person and show commitment by repetitiously going out on dates with him or her. Finally, the **third phase,** you will start to notice various changes in him or her for you have become complacent. Please note that many couples do well in the dating and mating game, but two out of three dating couples may not make it to the marital throne.

I know that many of you will disagree with my philosophy, but I ask you to look in retrospect and reexamine your past relationships especially the ones that caused you to experience emotional conflict. To the contrary of dating, courting has the potential to give an individual the time to check their cognitive behaviors for clarity and verity. The reason I put so much emphasis on courting for it is an old school term that derives from the South that holds no artificial scene (impressionable atmosphere). Courting will not necessarily lead one into temptation, but it will give you the opportunity to develop authentic emotions not built on sexual desires. Whereas, in dating the ultimate goal is to share physiological desert (sex), but most couples would deny that.

Courting

Courting is designed to express because it gives both parties the opportunity to learn each other's love style. A man feels courting is real since he does not have to pay to spend time with the lady of his interest, and his focus is on learning the blueprint of this person. Courting is powerful because the focus is on the spiritual side of the relationship. Some of the major characteristics of courting consist of going to the park and taking a stroll as you exchange philosophy about relationships and life in general. Many people who are in the courting phase spend a lot of time talking on the phone. Although, they cannot physically touch each other they can still develop a rapport. Also, the courting phase can oscillate between dating and courting depending on the development of their rapport.

The courting phase gives you ample time to gain trust with the person you are attracted to because sex is not your primary drive. When men and women can look at each other and not put emphasis on anatomical features, which is consistent with sexual fantasies, it allows you to tune in on each other's personality traits. Once couples lose trust in their relationship, they will seek emotional stability elsewhere. After this happens, your relationship is in checkmate (unable to grow). Therefore, it is important not to go into a relationship with a preconceived desire for the person you are searching for because it can set you up for relationship disappointment. The problem with this mindset you become caught up in the prejudging syndrome, which can cause the relationship to take a plunge. To prevent this one must take vital steps to develop a rewarding relationship.

Emotional Seed

In developing a relationship, the first step is called planting the emotional seed which is necessary for love to grow. The emotional seed sets the stage for emotional growth, and how do you do that? By staying on the spiritual side until you have developed social cohesiveness (the merging of each other). Maintaining a rapport takes time and requires emotional cultivation, and what do I mean by that? It means you make sure your person of interest is emotionally intact (free from past relationships that caused emotional trauma). Planting the emotional seed is important for it creates a trusting bond that can have longevity in your relationship. It is wise to be honest about your past relationships, so you do not make the same mistakes you made in previous relationships. I heavily advocate that men and women allow each other to feel safe with one another, if not; they will not disclose anything about themselves in an open manner.

The emotional seed is the foundation for growth and courting is the best way to accomplish this. To have a successful courtship, an individual should focus on learning a person's likes and dislikes. Once you have determined that your personalities are working in concert (together), then you can begin to nourish the emotional seed. In doing so, you can measure the growth of the relationship founded on genuine emotions, and it is then you will learn each other's morals, values, and belief system. It is a creative psychological process based on the meeting of the minds.

Emotional Nourishment

Emotional nourishment gives life to the seed of love, and without it, love cannot survive. What this involves is you must supply your person of interest with a mega dose of emotional vitamins. How do you do that? By sharing terms of endearment, administering ego food (compliments), showing a high level of respect, and exchanging philosophy about anything that pertains to the birth of your relationship. Also, giving gifts to represent your emotional desires and lastly, a simple hug or holding of hands is a high-tech form of what I call **emotional nourishment**. Remember if you deprive the emotional seed, it will expire in due time. To prevent the expiration of your relationship, keep it simple and do the moral thing. The only time a relationship becomes complicated is when the man or the woman is disrespecting, controlling, manipulative, self-centered, egotistical or downright selfish. Therefore, for emotional growth to occur, it is of utmost importance to consistently show respect for the man or woman you adore.

Emotional Pilot Light

The emotional pilot light is the nucleus of love because it keeps the glow in your relationship. When the pilot light goes out, it is an indicator that something is not right. Therefore, I strongly encourage you to keep your emotional pilot light well lit. The Webster Dictionary defines a relationship as a state of related or connected. What this means in simple terms is when you develop emotions for someone, you desire that person in a unique manner. Maintaining a level of respect for that individual is important. Otherwise, you will never develop into a complete union. In my view, the emotional pilot light is your love ruler because it measures your emotional progression. You must remember that light is the only defense for darkness. However, if the pilot light loses its glow, the relationship will move into total darkness, and when this happens, the relationship is over since the emotional pilot light is the fuel needed to maintain a rewarding and passionate relationship. Finally, when the pilot light is at the top of its glow, it is vital to uphold the eight essential love ingredients that are necessary for a successful relationship. If one of the ingredients is missing, the relationship will die.

Emotional Autopsy

Relationships can bring about pleasure or pain depending on the circumstances. For instance, when couples experience a great deal of emotional pain they are more apt to separate without fully explaining why they are parting and tend to allow the problem to lay dormant. When this happens, their relationship is suffering from a lack of emotional cohesiveness. It is not unusual for men and women to blame the other for the separation. For shifting the blame makes the transition easier to overcome guilt and shame, so one thinks.

The problem with this type of emotional transition is people tend to gravitate into a new relationship before thoroughly giving their prior relationship an **emotional autopsy**. Without understanding why your relationship failed you will subconsciously foster the same ills that you previously displayed in your past relationship.

Once you come to terms with why your relationship has deteriorated, you can begin the healing process. During this time, it is paramount not to get involved with anyone else until you are free of emotional trauma. Here's some food for thought, even if you grow out of love with your mate, you still need time to disassociate your entire gamut of emotions. Disconnecting makes it easier to enter into a new relationship with success for you are emotionally free and able to cultivate your heart to receive new emotional stimuli. A final note, you don't fall in love you grow in love, and it is a time-consuming process. As a result, one must incorporate my eight essential ingredients to have a successful relationship. In the next chapter, you will understand my vision and hopefully apply it to your next relationship. I believe my essential love ingredients are 99.9 pinpoint accurate, just keep reading, and you will appreciate what I am trying to convey.

For a relationship to be successful, it is paramount to utilize my eight essential love ingredients.

Respect
Honesty
Commitment
Human touch (intimacy)
Openness
Creativity
Communication
Love style

Eight Essential Love Ingredients

Do you know why so many relationships fail? It is reported two out of three relationships fail because men and women do not understand each other's love style. Couples use magical thinking when it comes to assuming what their companion desires. They should ask their partner what gives them joy and not assume for it may cause serious problems as your relationship progresses. One of the greatest deficits in a relationship is when couples move too fast and miss critical instructions. Earlier I mentioned the spiritual side of a relationship is where you learn the biology of real love. When you bypass this stage, you are without crucial knowledge of the emotional blueprint of your person of interest. Thus, I strongly advocate if you want a relationship that holds longevity, then it is wise to apply my emotional recipe. In doing so, you will notice the cohesive magic (the relationship is working) between the two of you that will guarantee joy, peace, and happiness. Therefore, I recommend that you follow my emotional blueprint and I promise you, you will discover the true art of this thing called, **love.** Are you ready to journey with me as I introduce you to the ingredients of my emotional relationship recipe? If so, then let's get busy!

Respect

The first emotional ingredient is **respect.** The Queen of Soul, Ms. Aretha Franklin stated, "**R.E.S.P.E.C.T** find out what it means to me," is pertinent to everyone. All human beings would love to be respected, but many couples do not understand the connotation of the word, respect. I am going to break these acronyms down step by step, so please pay close attention to my composing rhythm. Can you feel me?

R stands for **romance**. In many cases, if there is no finance there is no romance because the dating game cost money to create a romantic illusion. To the contrary, courting is the best way to display romantic attributes and gives both individuals the opportunity to reenergize the bylaws and importance of respecting each other's values, morals, and belief system. Based on my survey for this book and my practical application, if you do not respect yourself, you cannot respect your person of interest. So, you cannot love because love is simply to respect.

E stands for **eloquence**. When you respect someone you have honorable intentions, meaning your emotional expressions are clear, smooth, and heartfelt by making a conscious effort to make an individual feel safe.

S stands for **sensuous**. When you are talking to a person of interest, it is wise to shower that individual with high tech terms of endearments. It will arouse their entire gamut of emotions.

P stands for **passionate**. Being passionate is very exciting to women because they respond well to emotional stimuli. Showing emotions to your person of interest is always good for there is no defense for kindness. Women love men who are not afraid to show passion and vice versa for men.

E stands for **electrifying**. It is important for couples to recharge each other's gamut of emotions. Terms of endearments govern this type of emotional exchange.

C stands for **considerate**. Control and manipulation should not be a factor in a relationship for these two powers will destroy the cohesiveness of your social interactions. Instead, I suggest you think of your partner's interest as well as yours. It is vital to let your partner know that each other's well-being is equally praised.

T stands for **togetherness**. In relationships, the primary aim is to develop into a union filled with love, peace, joy and happiness. Men and women must play a significant role in orchestrating desirable intentions to accommodate their need for affection.

The above acronyms are designed to act as your emotional blueprint to guide you through your relationship. Bear in mind there is no defense for kindness as long as it is pure. Here's an example of how couples should show respect for each other.

John and April met each other one afternoon at a shopping mall. The two locked eyes as they were shopping in the same area for similar items. John, of course, was the aggressor because he walked over to April and asked her if she accepted compliments and April blushed and said, "of course I do." John then stated that she creates a beautiful illusion, and April replied, "thank you and what a lovely thing to say." John went on to ask if she would be kind enough to have lunch with him and April smiled and said, "I would love to." The opening statement to a person of interest must contain a high level of purity, displayed through linguistic and behavioral respect. Once an individual feels respected, they are more prone to surrender to what I call a smooth demonstration, showing holistic manners that will give one the desire to want more terms of endearment. All people require ego food, and without it, you will develop low self-esteem. Plus, it is an excellent social chess move. This type of interaction is the birth of developing a solid rapport that may have the potential for relationship growth.

Honesty

The second emotional ingredient is **honesty**. When couples are dishonest with each other, the relationship will slowly self-destruct. This behavior prevents an individual from developing a rapport that contains openness about self and other disturbing behaviors that might create some problems later in the relationship. When couples are not honest with each other, this usually stems from a powerful emotion called fear. It is hard to talk about past negative behaviors such as lying and cheating which caused a tremendous amount of guilt and shame in your past life. Nevertheless, if you are withholding something from your mate, it will eventually surface with a vengeance. When this happens, you can expect to lose some cohesiveness in your relationship. Therefore, I strongly suggest you disclose anything that may come back to haunt you later on in the relationship. All couples have made mistakes in their past relationships, but the key is, did they learn from them. Honesty can work to your advantage or work against you depending on the situation. Being honest in a relationship is the fuel that regulates your emotional pilot light. When honesty is missing from the equation of love, the relationship is doomed, so be as honest as possible with your mate.

Here's an example of what role honesty plays in a relationship. After having a delightful lunch together, John asked April if she would like to have dinner with him sometime soon and paint the town with meaningful social activities and April said yes! To make a long story short, the two went out to dinner the next weekend and had a marvelous time together. Do you recall in chapter two when I wrote about dating and courting, well unbeknownst, they are incorporating both styles? This segment of their rapport building was significant because it gave the two of them the opportunity to exchange philosophy about their lives and future endeavors and established a scene that was comfortable, classy and a quiet environment so they could penetrate each other's mindset. They were honest about answering questions the two of them had for each other. Fundamental questions such as, do you have any children, have you ever been married, do you have a degree, and what type of job do you have? Other subjects discussed were, what kind of car do you drive, where do you live, are you a native of Omaha, Nebraska, and many more questions about their social lives? These types of linguistic exchanges set the stage for emotional growth but keep in mind, every word you say will be eventually confirmed. Be **honest** then you don't have to worry about karma regarding dishonesty.

Commitment

The third emotional ingredient **commitment** is the aftermath of trust because if you do not trust your person of interest you will not be able to commit to him or her. In the relationship process, both individuals are sizing each other up to see if they are a match or not. Therefore, they watch every move they make and every step they take. When each feels their person of interest is trustworthy, they are more inclined to make an exclusive commitment to one another. Commitment is difficult if couples are not in touch with their gamut of emotions, and not knowing what their passion and purpose are in the relationship. If responsibility is absent from the relationship equation, relationship dishonesty is inevitable for many couples. To prevent this from occurring it is vital that couples establish the bylaws of commitment as soon as the relationship is in a safe place. Here's an example of two people who have made a commitment to each other.

After having an incredible time together, John and April decided to continue their relationship journey. They wanted to see each other on a regular basis because they enjoyed one another's company and that ignited their desire to be together. The two of them made a commitment not to see anyone else during their courting season. During this time, they were able to examine the moral fabric of their relationship and determine if they were of even yolk. By making a commitment, they established a unique bond which gave them the purpose to fulfill their emotional passion. Through this process, John and April were able to understand the guiding principles of commitment and moved onward.

Human Touch

The fourth emotional ingredient **human touch** has a distinct protocol for it welcomes intimacy. Most people think of intimacy as having a sexual relation which is a myth. Without human touch by the desired person, all of us would feel emotionally empty. Human touch has many flavors such as holding hands, giving each other a hug to represent closeness, the meeting of the lips, now that is straight up intimacy, huh? Most people do not feel safe being touched by a person they do not know. Therefore, it is important to build an intimate rapport before **passionate human touch** can occur. There are two forms of human touch, social and passionate. In most cases body language will describe what type of touch one is trying to display. A romantic touch happens when a person has an emotional desire for someone while a social touch has a friendly connotation to it. In relationships, touching is an extension of love, and it makes an individual feel desired in many ways. If this is missing in the equation of a relationship, bonding is nearly impossible for intimacy is the social glue that holds couples together. Be mindful; it takes little effort to reach out and touch somebody you care about since one of our strongest senses derives from human touch, besides, it's exciting!

John and April had experienced many dating and courting outings as they became familiar and comfortable with each other. Although this process is time-consuming, it is necessary for developing a healthy holistic relationship. Throughout their courting phase John would take April to the park for an evening stroll while holding hands to create intimacy and April welcomed the touching of her hands with open arms. Speaking of open arms, they began to give each other a passionate hug at the conclusion of each of their courtships. Human touch is significant since it creates a social intimacy that is paramount for the relationship to survive through this exciting period. It is vital that couples are consistent and persistent when it comes to human touch and without it, the relationship will move into emotional disparity. Lastly, I would like for you to acknowledge these two terms, tangible and intangible. Tangible is when you can physically reach out and touch your person of interest. On the other hand, intangible means you cannot physically touch your person of interest, but you can in a spiritual, cognitive manner and this happens through phone conversations. I just thought I would give you some mental food. Apparently, John and April have come to terms with the concept of human touch. It seems like they are doing the dang thang and that is what I'm talking about!

Openness

The fifth emotional ingredient is **openness.** As I stated in an earlier chapter, no one will disclose anything about themselves unless they have built a rapport with their person of interest. When that rapport is safely in place, only then they can become open to using logic. In a successful relationship, one cannot be closed minded because it will eventually cause the other party to shut completely down. Communication is the number one attribute all couples must have to maintain a positive relationship. When communication is tainted, many couples will lose their ability to indulge in active conversation with their person of interest, and this block the level of openness with their mate. As a result, the person is overwhelmed with fear and openness is not possible because of the consequences that derive from telling the truth. An introverted relationship can cause so many problems when sincerity is not present. To prevent this situation, I recommend you establish an extroverted relationship because the art of openness is naturally presented. Extroversion is a gregarious ingredient when both individuals are more apt to exchange philosophy more readily.

John and April's relationship is a classic example of how openness is implemented in a relationship. As their relationship continues to flourish, they have become very open with each other regarding the sharing of their emotions towards their new found relationship. April openly shared some past conflict she experienced with her ex-boyfriend. She expressed to John her ex-boyfriend hurt her by cheating on her with one of her best girlfriends. John noticed as she was talking about her ex-boyfriend she started to release some tears. Being the gentlemen that he is, handed her some napkins to wipe her beautiful eyes. John also stated, "If it is too painful to talk about your emotional pain, perhaps you shouldn't." April replied, "I am over him, but sometimes I get teary eyed when I think about how I allowed him to play me for a fool." She went on to say she wanted John to know her heart was well cultivated, and she is ready to move onward. John assured her openness about her previous relationship was a positive sign, and he appreciated her revealing how she felt regarding being hurt. Now that John feels comfortable with April, he gave her a big hug and told her she is in good hands, and his primary role in their relationship is to protect her from negative external stimuli. It is a prime example of how openness can ease the pain of past conflicts. When couples are open with each other, it acts similar to a safety net that allows them to feel secured in disclosing painful memories.

Creativity

The sixth emotional ingredient is **creativity.** Routine assignment (repetitive behavior) is one of the biggest deficits in a relationship. A healthy relationship should contain two primary entities, innovation and of course creativity. A routine assignment can cause relationship boredom, and when this happens, the relationship suffers immensely. One of the ways to prevent this from happening is to be creative not only during the dating and mating phase but throughout the course of your relationship. One has to be willing to try new exciting adventures and not be afraid of failure. Most couples become too complacent in their relationships and find it easier to remain in their comfort zone. Unbeknownst, sooner or later boredom will conquer the relationship, and when this happens, the union of the relationship slowly but surely self-destruct if there is no acknowledgment from both parties of the problem. Creativity is very powerful in a relationship because it can be stimulating and rewarding to the soul of the relationship. You may be wondering what is meant by creativity. For instance, the changing of social schedules can arouse your gamut of emotions. Plan out your social schedule with your mate and revise it weekly by being innovative with your schedule. Creativity is not exclusively for social activity, but it is also wise to be creative in the bedroom as well for when boredom sets in that particular room, the relationship is in serious trouble. For real! I expect you will use your imagination to incorporate new ideas to support your emotional attachment to your person of interest. Trust me; you don't want sexual boredom to set in for if it does, infidelity will most likely occur. So, remember that change means growth and if you cannot grow you will not make that change.

John and April are having a ball in their courting and dating phase because they are both willing to participate in activities out of the ordinary to arouse their impeccable desire for each other. In doing so, boredom in their relationship doesn't stand a chance. When a couple first meet it is an electrifying moment for the two of them, but as time progresses something happens and what do you think that is? If you recall, routine assignment brings about dullness and the only antidote for that is creativity. John and April understood this concept and made a conscious effort to avoid doing the same activities redundantly during their courtship. They used laughter as a brilliant mechanism to keep joy alive in their relationship. One week they may go to a movie, the following week they are strolling in the park and finally settling down to enjoy a nice picnic together or walking through the snow counting snowflakes. It is an excellent example of how creativity can enhance a relationship. There are many social events new couples can engage in, but one must remember, the same thing it took to get him or her it will require the same effort to maintain the relationship. Thus far John and April are experiencing a high level of excitement. If they can achieve social ecstasy, so can you!

Communication

Relationship experts state communication between two people is the crazy glue that holds it all together, and without the ability to communicate effectively, a relationship will slowly self-destruct. Out of all the emotional ingredients **communication** is by far the most important since it gives a couple a chance to learn the dynamics of each other's morals, values, and belief system. Many couples have the propensity to shut down because they feel the other party is not listening to their cry. When couples have trouble communicating, it means that one of them is trying to manipulate and control the other person. Technically, it is a form of menticide (brainwashing). When communication is intact, it creates a strong union, for it allows both individuals to feel safe, respected, but most of all, appreciated.

Love Styles

The eighth and final emotional ingredient is your **love style.** For the proceeding ingredients to work, you must first establish your love style. If you do not know what your love style is, you will by the end of this chapter. Love style refers to what type of social emotional-style you present to your person of interest. What does social-emotional style mean? It means you are an introvert, extrovert or ambivert. Now you are probably wondering what the heck that is? Well, I will break each style down for you so you can determine which one are you. Let's get busy!

The **introvert love style** is one who keeps their emotions inward. This love style is complex because this person does not express their emotions in an open manner. Therefore, their mate is constantly wondering what this individual is feeling. Introverts are very settled and observe everything within their circumference. They are more apt to allow their emotions to simmer until specific stimuli elicit a reaction or a response. In the relationship process, introverts tend to use what I call magical thinking (assuming what their mate is thinking) which can create serious problems in their relationship. This particular love style doesn't work very well with another introvert love style because they tend to misconstrue each other. The love style requires an enormous amount of probing; otherwise, they will not readily disclose their emotions.

Relationships require communication, a matter of fact, if there is no communication the relationship becomes stagnant. Introverts are not communicators; they are usually thinkers who ponder on their emotions but do not express them to their person of interest. For instance, when introverts go out on a date, they may appear to be shy, but in actuality, they want to exchange emotional philosophy but feel linguistically incompetent. When they don't articulate, this is mind trickery because the mate of the introvert does not know which way to go regarding conversation. Introverts are more prone to date an extrovert, and they rely on their partner's emotional input and echo their conversation. Have you ever been on a date and noticed your partner was relatively silent? They may give the impression they are bored, but in reality, they are displaying introvert characteristics.

The **extrovert love style** contains emotional expression, and they are naturally socially expressive. Many extroverts are histrionic (attention seekers), therefore; they are more likely to express themselves in an aggressive manner and are in tune with their emotional expressions. Extroverts do not allow their emotions to simmer when something is unclear to them, and they will confront the issue. In a relationship, extroverts are very communicative and willingly share their feelings with their person of interest. The extrovert love style works best with an introvert for they are opposite of each other because the extrovert will elicit conversation with the introvert love style. They share their emotions candidly which can create relationship growth given the two of them are working towards the same emotional goal, which is building a positive rapport that has the potential to modulate into **love.**

An example of an extrovert love style is when both individuals have equal emotional input towards one another, and they piggyback off each other's emotions. In doing so, they become each other's emotional student, and this occurs through active listening. Unlike the introvert love style, extroverts enjoy exchanging philosophy about everything related to their relationship. Lastly, the extrovert love style has a greater capacity to take their relationship to the marital throne since they both have reached the apex of their gamut of emotions.

The **ambivert love style** is unique for it can oscillate between the introvert and extrovert love styles. What does this entail? It merely means an ambivert can unite with both love styles depending on the level of their desire for that person of interest. Ambiverts are well-adapted people because they have the potential to interact romantically with an introvert or extrovert love style. They tend to be open and honest about what they want in a relationship and are not afraid to extend themselves emotionally. Many people may not be aware that ambiverts are the most respected individuals in the dating and courtship paradigm, for they are not judgmental towards their person of interest. For the most part, they will look at their relationship through unconditional lens.

When John and April first met the two of them hit it off right away because John is an extrovert and April is an ambivert. They were able to connect with each other's love style since they had similar characteristics and openly exchanged emotional philosophy with one another. It was an excellent start for them as their love styles complimented each other.

Warning!!! Introverts tend to do better with an extrovert, and ambiverts can accommodate both love styles, but introverts do not do well with another introvert. Therefore, it is wise to be mindful of which love style is appropriate for you for if you choose the wrong love style you can move into emotional disparity, trust me!

The three love styles are essential in developing a relationship for if they clash, the beginning of the relationship will be difficult to maintain. Keep in mind people are not what they appear to be when you first meet them, but as time progresses, you will know if they are authentic or not. It is why I strongly advocate you spend ample time on the spiritual side of the relationship since this is where you will discover if you are of even yolk or not. Relationships tend to move too fast and become preoccupied with the dessert of the relationship, which is sex. Otherwise, sex without emotions is nothing but gymnastics. Nevertheless, if you want your relationship to work, I encourage you to pay close attention to the vital steps I have recommended. These steps have been tested and will act as your emotional blueprint that will possibly carry you to the marital throne.

The Merging of the Hearts (Marriage)

Have you ever heard people say they have met their soul mate, and it was love at first sight? Wow! It is an interesting concept because love is truly an act of progression that requires a specific amount of time. Most people who make this statement are conveying their person of interest arouses them. In my opinion, they got it twisted as love does not usually work that way. However, some couples insist their relationship was love at first sight. How can it be when you had not planted the **emotional seed?** In the second chapter, I stated you have to cultivate the emotional soil and then plant the emotional seed. Then and only then can you begin to nourish the emotional seed which requires time to illuminate. In the first stage of emotional growth, you are caught up in an emotional maze filled with mythical thinking (things that are not true).

Couples have the tendency to ignore vital clues that will determine if their chemistry is in harmony with each other. Usually, this occurs when their external illusion is greater than the internal illusion. You are probably wondering what is meant by this statement. Well, we live in a cute society, and we are prone to search for perfection. Once couples feel they have met their match, they will move to the next step, which is marriage. After they get married, the couple believes their relationship will last forever, but only time will tell. Afterward, they are overwhelmed with the excitement of being married because everything appears to be right. But, they don't have a clue about what can happen after the honeymoon phase. Let's examine the honeymoon phase and hopefully you readers who are married may be able to identify with some of the problems that occur during this crucial phase.

The Honeymoon Phase

The marital phase could be very misleading if the relationship missed vital steps at the beginning of the relationship. In this stage, couples feel safe in each other's arms because they love their human touch. This relationship phase is exciting and emotionally charged with passion and gratification that satisfies their emotional and sexual desires. Couples usually cannot take their eyes off of each other for long periods without craving for their presence. The dessert of their relationship is filled with joyful experiences that allow the two of them to merge and have psychological, emotional, and sexual orgasms. Wow! That sounds amazing, doesn't it? Also, this phase of the marriage will determine if the relationship holds promise because the excitement doesn't necessarily last for long. Relationship therapist states the honeymoon phase last anywhere from one to five or more years before noticing emotional changes that may or may not affect their marriage. One noticeable characteristic is the excitement of being together becomes routine assignment. Let's take a commercial and examine how John and April are during thus far in their relationship.

John and April became engaged and eventually married after approximately one year. They went on their honeymoon and enjoyed each other to the fullest. When they returned from their honeymoon, they began to start a beautiful life together. Their communication level was respectful, and they continuously gave each other ego food which is necessary for relationship grooming. Relationships work when couples communicate effectively with each other, and John and April have mastered their ability to do just that. So far, their relationship is without internal conflict. That's what I'm talking about.

Marital Longevity

Marital longevity refers to the duration of the marriage. It is important to understand if marriage is going to have longevity, both individuals must recognize their marital bylaws. The eight essential love ingredients discussed earlier are the emotional blueprint for a successful marriage. In reality, it is the social glue that holds the marriage together. When one of these ingredients are missing from the relationship equation, it threatens marital longevity. As mentioned in my introduction, two out of three relationships fail, the question is why? Marriages are failing miserably for various reasons, but specifically, it is due to a lack of communication. The biggest arguments that occur in a marriage is about money, disrespect, infidelity, lack of compassion, controlling and manipulative behaviors, lack of trust, and most importantly the inability to understand each other's love style.

Marriages that maintain longevity is because they respect each other's independence and value each other as a human being. When needs are unmet in a marital relationship, the emotional seed will die. In a marriage when couples are auguring the majority of the time, it is due to one or the other trying to dominate the other person to accept their ideology. After so long, either the husband or the wife will say, "that's it, I cannot do this anymore." Usually, when this happens, one of them will leave their home to find peace, and if there are children involved, this can be devastating for them. Legal separation can have a positive outcome depending on if there is therapeutic intervention, but in most cases, there is not.

Marital Separation

Separation occurs when the husband and wife can no longer tolerate each other's nonsense. Couples who separate without thoroughly understanding why tend to remain apart. It is important to note that absence grows fonder to the heart, but it can also grow away from the heart depending on how they are communicating during their separation. Other reasons for marital separation is frustration, resentment, anger, disappointment, hurt, and a black heart (not showing affection). It also includes sexual incompetence, lack of money to support their lifestyle, and lastly but most importantly, a lack of mutual respect for each other. The list can go on and on, and these causations are more than enough to cause one to say, "I am tired of trying." How can two people who say they love each other and have so many marital problems? It is a clear indication that somewhere within their dating and courting phase, couples ignored vital clues. Once separation is in place, it is wise for both individuals to apply the **cause and effect theory.** It appears for every action there is a reaction for one person is never solely at fault for the separation since it takes two people to ignite this type of marital explosion. It is why I encourage couples to utilize my TSC Format which entails **target, source, and change**. During the separation, I suggest both individuals find the target of their conflict (who are you angry with), next they need to discover the source of their problems (why are you angry), and then determine if this is something that you can change. If you can change it, then design a master plan to modify your negative behavior, so you learn how to accommodate each other's belief system. Otherwise, if you cannot change the situation, then they should not give their emotional deficits any power because if they continue to do so, their relationship will certainly crumble.

On the other hand, when couples separate, and can discuss their differences in a healthy manner, their relationship is usually salvageable. Although this is a time-consuming process, it is achievable if both parties are willing to work towards the reunion of their marriage. Upon the reunion of married couples who have experienced marital separation, it is paramount the two of them work harder than previously to maintain a constant flow of respect for each other. Relationships are very sensitive to negative stimuli, and therefore, it is wise to step outside of your box and reexamine your moral fabric and extend yourself with sheer passion towards your significant other. Remember, the same thing it took to get him or her it must be duplicated to maintain the relationship.

The Departing of the Hearts (Divorce)

When couples reunite after a short or lengthy separation, they must begin to think methodically and approach their marriage with caution for they are very sensitive to each other's past behavior.

After a separation, it is hard to reenergize the relationship, but it is possible if the two are working faithfully to overcome their differences. Infidelity is not easy to overcome in marriage since the level of trust has been severely damaged. When this occurs, I suggest the couple apply the **cause and effect theory** since something drove the husband or wife to search for emotional stability elsewhere. Relationship therapist believes couples can rekindle their relationship even though their trust level is morally defunct. In my opinion, once a person breaks the trust, it is not easy to regain. My reason for stating this is because the mate that was faithful will always wonder what their partner is doing when they are apart. It can be very distracting in the relationship due to a preoccupation of dishonesty. Even though both individuals are trying hard to conquer their marital deficits, it is still a challenge to manage. A marriage filled with frustration, anger, resentment and a lack of human touch, means the emotional seed has expired. Although the marital script states "to death do us part," many couples fall short of understanding this concept.

When couples decide to divorce, and they have children, it can be very painful for not only the husband and wife but for the children as well. As soon as the divorce is final, it is vital that both individuals give their relationship an **emotional autopsy** before they move onward with another prospect. If they don't complete a thorough emotional autopsy, they will carry the same mistakes into their next relationship, and this isn't good. Lastly, be mindful that change brings about growth.

Have you ever wondered why people get married more than two times during their lifetime? Well, it has a lot to do with finding the right love style, and that is why many people are having trouble understanding the reasons why they keep making the same mistakes in their relationship. My purpose for composing this book is to give the reader my recipe for a successful marriage. I hope you readers find stability in your future relationships.

The Final Call for Relationship Change

Many people fear change because they do not know what to expect, but what they need to know is change means growth, therefore, without change, you cannot grow. As stated throughout the course of this book, relationships are not complicated. Instead, people make it difficult because they move too fast into a relationship based on external illusion and this must stop for substance is greater than appearance. I strongly suggest every human being take a moral inventory (the principles of what is right or wrong) on a regular basis to stay in touch with your heated soul.

You must find your passion and purpose of this thing called life to live it without excessive emotional trauma. However, as long as you are exchanging oxygen you will encounter some problems, but the key is what you are going to do about it. You have to stop blaming others for your shortcomings and learn to look at the man or the woman in the mirror. When you are in the process of developing a relationship, you must be open minded and have a high level of respect for one another. Relationships can be beautiful if individuals learn to communicate with each other and not put one another down. It is sad when relationships fail before they reach relationship maturity. What happens with relationships, they become too complacent and don't allow change to occur. The bottom line is, you must learn to "accept the things you cannot change and change the things you can, and have the wisdom to know the difference." Please remember, the only person you can change is the person you were yesterday.

Prescription for Relationship Integrity

Couples are having problems understanding what relationship integrity means. Misconstruing relationship values causes problems

33

to surface, and when this happens, the relationship is in serious trouble. Marital bylaws govern successful relationships, and when honesty, commitment, and open conversation are missing from the relationship, the emotional foundation will collapse. Integrity is vital for it holds the values together and without integrity, it is almost impossible to sustain a healthy relationship. Once respect for the relationship is damaged, it minimizes the ability to communicate effectively. If this occurs, the couple will eventually stop talking to each other and avoid as much contact as possible. I call this the **black heart syndrome** (inability to show emotions), and at this point, the level of integrity has vanished. Let's examine how to maintain integrity within a relationship. First of all, you have to value yourself before you can value someone else. Integrity to a relationship is what gasoline is to a car for it gives the relationship upward mobility.

In psychology, there is a word called **affect**. It is when your verbal expression does not match your facial expression, and it means something is not right! But, don't forget people learn to mimic well and master the art of deception. It is why I put so much emphasis on the spiritual side of a relationship for this is where substance lies. When couples merge, they bring three different flavors to the union, morals, values, and beliefs. It is important both individuals have a mega dose of respect for each other. As I stated before, you cannot change another person, but you can make a change within yourself. It is very healthy to accept a person for whom and what they represent in a relationship. What usually happens in relationships is one or the other is trying to mold their person of interest into their mindset, and this is called menticide (brainwashing).

Relationship ignorance is having no knowledge of how a relationship should work. Do you fully understand the definition of integrity, and if so, was it implemented in your relationship? In my arena of life coaching, many of my clients who are experiencing marital conflict state their relationship has lost the element of integrity. So, why do couples lose respect for each other? Let's stop for a minute, for I would like for you to look in retrospect and reexamine your past or present relationship to determine if you valued the relationship. Next, I would like for you to ask yourself did your partner value the relationship. It is important to show your mate in a repetitious manner you respect and value their opinion. However, I believe most couples, in the beginning, value their relationship but as time progresses either the man or woman will shut down if they are not appreciated, and this isn't good! There are ways of letting your mate know they are the nucleus (center piece) of the relationship. In doing so, you will discover there is no defense for positive ego food. Wow, how about that! If you are presently in a relationship, value it because the best gift two people can give each other is self. Let's check in on John and April's relationship progression.

John and April's relationship contains integrity, honesty, openness, and respect. They are doing very well in their marriage and loving every minute of their offspring. April is so amazed how her husband respects her and listens to her every word without hesitation. That's what I am talking about, for you men who are reading this book, please listen when your woman needs to talk. Remember, a women's greatest complaint about most men is they don't listen. John is intellectually well groomed, in terms of regarding his maturity for he understands his wife and cherishes her existence. The reason their marriage is so successful is both of them are well-balanced individuals who realize the bylaws of pure unconditional love. I strongly suggest you follow John and April's example and step outside of your box to extend your arms with conviction and when you do that your husband or wife will know their love for you is not in vain.

Be the Best that You Can Be

If you rise above your environment, the universe will meet you. What this metaphor entails is if you give life every iota of you, you are successful because you have no more to give. Once you thoroughly understand happiness is about giving and not receiving, you can begin to witness the beauty of exchanging oxygen. In relationships, it is your time to shine and show the world and your mate what you have to offer. One of the greatest gifts on earth is the ability to love unconditionally. To the contrary, many people have problems with differentiating between conditional and unconditional love. Conditional love is not true love for it is designed to focus on specific characteristics of your partner. On the other hand, unconditional love is to respect, honor and appreciate the positive and negative characteristics of your mate. Unconditional love is not biased or selfish it is pure. It is not controlling or manipulative or self-centered, it is the sunshine of your soul. Many people use the term love too loosely because when you love someone, you do not hurt them intentionally.

Another term widely used is I am **sorry.** The term sorry should only be used when an accident occurs not an incident as there is a major difference between the two terms. In relationships, the husband or wife may hurt each other and say they are sorry, but how can this be when your actions were not accidental, come on now! Human beings have been programmed to use the term sorry to erase their guilt and shame when they are at fault. Why would you accept someone saying I am sorry for something that was premeditated? When you learn to **be the best that you can be** and stay within the circumference of morality, sorry is used to raise the consciousness of an accident. So if you have hurt your mate and it was not an accident, don't say that you are sorry, apologize for your negative behavior. And finally, when someone executes an incident towards you, and they say I am sorry, tell them to get on with that inappropriate noise. For once you learn to be the best that you can be, your shadow will envy you.

I want you all to know I sincerely care about the general welfare of your relationships, and I wish you all the happiness in your near and far future. I hope this reality book tapped into your soul and ignited your moral system to the degree where you take a moral inventory and reexamine your relationship before it is too late. The failure of two out of three relationships is a terrible situation to be in, for you are better than that! So, I ask you why do human beings argue, fuss, and fight, then turn right around and makeup only to break up?

Oh, guess what? John and April have been married for over 40 years. Their emotional seed is well nourished and has an everlasting glow in their emotional pilot light. Remember, relationships depart because the emotional seed suffers from a severe form of emotional neglect. Therefore, when a desire is missing from the emotional equation, motivation is absent. I have been a faithful warner. . . **Ciao Bella!**

I love you and thank you for your undivided attention.

Dr. Jeffery L. Walker

★ Books ★

I think you'll love reading these two books

Go to drjefferyvision4change.net and order a copy today!

Printed in the United States
By Bookmasters